The Glorious Quran

True Guidance from Allah

Easy English Translation
Juz 24

(From Surah Az-Zummar to Surah Ghaafir)
(From Surah 39 to Surah 40)

Translated by

Mohammad Ali Khan

Copyrights © Mohammad Ali Khan 2024

All rights reserved.

All rights reserved. No part of this publication may be reproduced, distributed, or transmitted in any form or by any means, including photocopying, recording, or other electronic or mechanical methods, without the author's prior written permission, except in the case of brief quotations embodied in critical reviews and certain other non-commercial uses permitted by copyright law. For permission requests, please get in touch with the author.

Dedication	1
Acknowledgments	2
About the Author	3
Preface	4
سُوْرَةُ الزُّمَرِ	6
Surah Az-Zummar	6
The Glorious Quran Surah 39	6
سورة غافر	23
Surah Ghaafir	23
The Glorious Quran 40	23

Dedication

Dedicated to all souls out there looking for the ultimate truth and ultimate guidance.

Acknowledgments

This simple translation was sent to many friends for feedback and corrections. I am really thankful and acknowledge the efforts of Dr. Syed Shafiq Ur Rahman of Florida, Mr. Muzaffar Sheikh of Florida, Mr. Nasir Awan of Delaware, and Dr. Farrukh Azmi of North Carolina for corrections and feedback.

About the Author

Mohammad Ali Khan, a pediatrician by profession, loves to read the Holy Quran and enjoys the way it is recited and the way it sounds. He proclaims and pronounces Allah as the only Creator and the only God worthy of worship. He believes in prophet Muhammad peace be upon him as true and the final messenger of Allah. He believes that explanation of the Quran is only acceptable if it is from another part of the Quran or from the authentic hadith narrated from prophet Muhammad peace be upon him. Unauthentic stories from literature and history books must be avoided as an explanation of the Quran. Teachings of Quran as explained by prophet Muhammad peace be upon him, take human beings out from worshiping personalities, idols, wealth, self interest, family interest, tribal interests, national interest, arrogance, self-worship, and self-praise. Quran takes human beings into total obedience to Allah and his prophet peace be upon him.

Preface

The Holy Quran has many translations in almost every language of the world. Sometimes, the meaning is confused, or the beauty of the scripture is lost in the translation. Sometimes, one word can not describe the meaning of the original word in the text.

The words of the Holy Quran are forever, not changeable, unique, and nothing is like these words anywhere in the world and no one can bring anything forward like this ever. The author thinks that translation should correspond to these words of the original text.

The meaning given to words of the Holy Quran can only be explained by the prophet Muhammad (peace be upon him). Any other explanation that is not reported or connected to the prophet (peace be upon him) or his companions (may Allah be pleased with all of them) may be the personal opinion of that person.

This simple translation is different in a few ways.

1. Meanings should correspond to the original words as closely as possible.

2. All pronouns should be explained as to whom those pronouns are referring to.

3. If one meaning is not doing justice to the original word, alternatives should be mentioned.

4. Meanings should be simple and easy to understand for common people.

5. Paraphrasing the meaning of the Quran should be avoided with an injection of thoughts and words not supported by the original text of the Glorious Quran.

6. Personal thoughts should be kept away; the words of Allah are enough for guidance.

7. Names of prophets should be mentioned as mentioned in the Quran with the same name and spelling mentioned in the Glorious Quran, not as mentioned elsewhere.

8. Reference from other books and history must be avoided especially narrative mentioned in Christian and Jewish literature. The authenticity of those narratives and stories can not be confirmed.

9. The only reference acceptable is from Prophet Muhammad (peace be upon him) or his companions in the form of Sahih Hadith.

10. References from the scholars of later centuries, other than the explanation given by prophet Muhammad peace be upon him and his companions, are just their personal opinions. Those personal opinions may or may not be correct.

11. Scientific narrative must be kept away as those scientific facts may change with time, and the glorious Quran is not for the purpose of explaining science.

12. This book, the glorious Quran, is for all people, all generations till the day of judgment; new information available to current and future generations may help explain the word of the Quran better, as mentioned by prophet Muhammad (peace be upon him).

13. Personal explanations and opinions given by earlier scholars are not part of the original text, and this difference must be kept in mind.

14. Any extra explanation to make the meaning clear and easy is given in parenthesis and is not part of the original text. This difference must be kept in mind.

To connect with the author, Mohammad Ali Khan, please email shahab35@hotmail.com, phone 443-350-2359, Whatsapp 014433502359, X (formerly known as Twitter) account @khanmohammadali, hashtag #easyQuran.

Any guidance, comment or criticism from any person around the world regarding words and the accuracy of its meaning is highly appreciated. Any comment or suggestion will be replied to as much as possible.

سُوْرَةُ الزُّمَرِ

Surah Az-Zummar

The Glorious Quran Surah 39

بِسْمِ اللَّهِ الرَّحْمَٰنِ الرَّحِيمِ

(I begin) with the name of Allah, the Most Kind (the Most Beneficent), the Most Merciful

Aya 39:1

تَنزِيلُ الْكِتَابِ مِنَ اللَّهِ الْعَزِيزِ الْحَكِيمِ

Revelation of the book (Quran) is from Allah, the All-Mighty, the All-Wise.

Aya 39:2

إِنَّا أَنزَلْنَا إِلَيْكَ الْكِتَابَ بِالْحَقِّ فَاعْبُدِ اللَّهَ مُخْلِصًا لَّهُ الدِّينَ

Surely. We (Allah), sent down (revealed) We (Allah), toward you (O prophet Muhammad, peace be upon him) the book (Quran) on the truth, so worship Allah, making pure (sincere, exclusive) for Him (for Allah) the Deen (religion, worship, the way of life)

Aya 39:3

أَلَا لِلَّهِ الدِّينُ الْخَالِصُ وَالَّذِينَ اتَّخَذُوا مِن دُونِهِ أَوْلِيَاءَ مَا نَعْبُدُهُمْ إِلَّا لِيُقَرِّبُونَا إِلَى اللَّهِ زُلْفَىٰ إِنَّ اللَّهَ يَحْكُمُ بَيْنَهُمْ فِي مَا هُمْ فِيهِ يَخْتَلِفُونَ إِنَّ اللَّهَ لَا يَهْدِي مَنْ هُوَ كَاذِبٌ كَفَّارٌ

Beware, (only) for Allah is the Deen (religion, worship), the pure (sincere and exclusive Deen) and those who took (made) from besides Him (Allah) friends (protectors, guardians), (saying) not we worship them (those gods other than Allah) except for, they (those partners gods) will make us nearer toward Allah (in) nearness, surely, Allah will decide between them (disbelievers who make partners with Allah) in what they were in it (issue of Oneness of Allah) differing, surely, Allah does not guide (to the right path) the one who is (a) liar, severe rejector (ungrateful, disbeliever)

Aya 39:4

لَّوْ أَرَادَ اللَّهُ أَن يَتَّخِذَ وَلَدًا لَّاصْطَفَىٰ مِمَّا يَخْلُقُ مَا يَشَاءُ سُبْحَانَهُ هُوَ اللَّهُ الْوَاحِدُ الْقَهَّارُ

If wanted Allah, that He takes (makes) a son, definitely, He (Allah) would have chosen (as a son) from what He (Allah) creates, what He (Allah) wanted (willed), purity (pure and above is Allah from having a son) is for Him (for Allah), He is Allah, the Only One, the One (Allah, with) extreme power of punishment.

Aya 39:5

خَلَقَ السَّمَاوَاتِ وَالْأَرْضَ بِالْحَقِّ يُكَوِّرُ اللَّيْلَ عَلَى النَّهَارِ وَيُكَوِّرُ النَّهَارَ عَلَى اللَّيْلِ وَسَخَّرَ الشَّمْسَ وَالْقَمَرَ كُلٌّ يَجْرِي لِأَجَلٍ مُّسَمًّى أَلَا هُوَ الْعَزِيزُ الْغَفَّارُ

He (Allah) created the skies (heavens) and the earth with the truth, He (Allah) rolls (folds) the night on the day and He (Allah) rolls (folds) the day on the night and He (Allah) made subservient (obedient) the sun and the moon, all (sun and moon and everything) run for appointed time, named (known), beware, He (Allah) is the All-Mighty the Most-Forgiver.

Aya 39:6

خَلَقَكُم مِّن نَّفْسٍ وَاحِدَةٍ ثُمَّ جَعَلَ مِنْهَا زَوْجَهَا وَأَنزَلَ لَكُم مِّنَ الْأَنْعَامِ ثَمَانِيَةَ أَزْوَاجٍ يَخْلُقُكُمْ فِي بُطُونِ أُمَّهَاتِكُمْ خَلْقًا مِّن بَعْدِ خَلْقٍ فِي ظُلُمَاتٍ ثَلَاثٍ ذَٰلِكُمُ اللَّهُ رَبُّكُمْ لَهُ الْمُلْكُ لَا إِلَٰهَ إِلَّا هُوَ فَأَنَّىٰ تُصْرَفُونَ

He (Allah) created you from nafs (person) one (from one individual meaning prophet Adam peace be upon him), then He (Allah) made from it (from the body of that nafs, that person) pair (wife) of it, and He sent down (created) for you from the cattle, eight pairs, He (Allah) creates you in the bellies of mothers of yours, creation from after creation in darknesses three, that (for) you, is Allah, Lord of yours, (only) for Him (Allah) is the kingdom, not is there any one worthy of worship except Him (Allah) so where are you turned away (diverted away from the truth)

Aya 39:7

إِن تَكْفُرُوا فَإِنَّ اللَّهَ غَنِيٌّ عَنكُمْ وَلَا يَرْضَىٰ لِعِبَادِهِ الْكُفْرَ وَإِن تَشْكُرُوا يَرْضَهُ لَكُمْ وَلَا تَزِرُ وَازِرَةٌ وِزْرَ أُخْرَىٰ ثُمَّ إِلَىٰ رَبِّكُم مَّرْجِعُكُمْ فَيُنَبِّئُكُم بِمَا كُنتُمْ تَعْمَلُونَ إِنَّهُ عَلِيمٌ بِذَاتِ الصُّدُورِ

If you (all) reject (become ungrateful to Allah), so surely, Allah is Self-Sufficient (Carefree, not in need) from you (all creations), and not He (Allah) approves for servants of His (Allah) the disbelief (rejection of faith,, ungratefulness) and if you practice gratefulness He (Allah) approves it (the gratefulness) for you, and does not bear (carry the burden or is responsible) a bearer (carrier of sins, a person) the burden (of sins) of the other (person), then toward Lord of yours (Allah) is the place of return of yours, so He (Allah) will inform you, on what you were doing (in the worldly life), surely, He (Allah) is the All-Knower on the owners of the chests (what is in hearts of people)

Aya 39:8

وَإِذَا مَسَّ الْإِنْسَانَ ضُرٌّ دَعَا رَبَّهُ مُنِيبًا إِلَيْهِ ثُمَّ إِذَا خَوَّلَهُ نِعْمَةً مِّنْهُ نَسِيَ مَا كَانَ يَدْعُو إِلَيْهِ مِن قَبْلُ وَجَعَلَ لِلَّهِ أَندَادًا لِّيُضِلَّ عَن سَبِيلِهِ قُلْ تَمَتَّعْ بِكُفْرِكَ قَلِيلًا إِنَّكَ مِنْ أَصْحَابِ النَّارِ

And when touched the human being harm, he (human) called (invoked, prayed to) Lord of his (Allah) returner (coming back sincerely) toward Him (Allah), then when He (Allah) bestowed on (gave) him (the human) giving (grace, bounty, health, money and wealth) from (the grace of) Him (Allah) he (human being) forgot what he was praying (invoking, calling) toward Him (Allah) from before, and he (human being) made for Allah equals (partners as false gods), for him (human being) to misguide (other people) from the path of His (Allah), Say (O prophet Muhammad peace be upon him): take benefit (enjoy the advantage a) little (small benefit and temporarily), surely, you are from the companions of the fire

Aya 39:9

أَمَّنْ هُوَ قَانِتٌ آنَاءَ اللَّيْلِ سَاجِدًا وَقَائِمًا يَحْذَرُ الْآخِرَةَ وَيَرْجُو رَحْمَةَ رَبِّهِ قُلْ هَلْ يَسْتَوِي الَّذِينَ يَعْلَمُونَ وَالَّذِينَ لَا يَعْلَمُونَ إِنَّمَا يَتَذَكَّرُ أُولُو الْأَلْبَابِ

Is the one who is devoutly obedient (that person is, in) periods of the night prostrating and standing (in prayers to Allah, during hours of the night), he fears the hereafter, and he is hoping (for) mercy of Lord of his (Allah, is that obedient person equal to disobeying rejectors)? Say (O prophet Muhammad peace be upon him), are equal those who know and those who do not know? Surely (truth is) that take remembrance (accept reminder, take advice) owners of the wit (persons with intelligence, understanding)

39:10

قُلْ يَا عِبَادِ الَّذِينَ آمَنُوا اتَّقُوا رَبَّكُمْ لِلَّذِينَ أَحْسَنُوا فِي هَذِهِ الدُّنْيَا حَسَنَةٌ وَأَرْضُ اللَّهِ وَاسِعَةٌ إِنَّمَا يُوَفَّى الصَّابِرُونَ أَجْرَهُم بِغَيْرِ حِسَابٍ

Say (O prophet Muhammad peace be upon him), O, servants of Mine (Allah) those who believed (in Allah), fear Lord of yours (Allah), for those who did good deeds in this world, (any) good deed (will be fully rewarded), and the earth of Allah is spacious (so immigrate to where you can worship only One Allah), surely (truth is) that, will be fully rewarded the (people who are) patients, reward of theirs without accounts (limits, measures)

Aya 39:11
قُلْ إِنِّي أُمِرْتُ أَنْ أَعْبُدَ اللَّهَ مُخْلِصًا لَّهُ الدِّينَ

Say (O prophet Muhammad, peace be upon him): surely, I am ordered (commanded by Allah) that I worship Allah, making pure (sincere, exclusive) for Him (for Allah) Deen (religion, worship, way of life)

Aya 39:12
وَأُمِرْتُ لِأَنْ أَكُونَ أَوَّلَ الْمُسْلِمِينَ

And I am ordered (commanded by Allah), for that I become first of the Muslims (obedient, submitting myself to the orders of Allah)

Aya 39:13
قُلْ إِنِّي أَخَافُ إِنْ عَصَيْتُ رَبِّي عَذَابَ يَوْمٍ عَظِيمٍ

Say (O prophet Muhammad, peace be upon him), surely, I fear if I disobeyed Lord of mine (Allah), punishment of the day great (big day of judgment)

Aya 39:14
قُلِ اللَّهَ أَعْبُدُ مُخْلِصًا لَّهُ دِينِي

Say (O prophet Muhammad, peace be upon him), (only One) Allah, I worship, making pure (sincere, exclusive) for Him (Allah) Deen (religion, worship, way of life) of mine.

Aya 39:15
فَاعْبُدُوا مَا شِئْتُم مِّن دُونِهِ قُلْ إِنَّ الْخَاسِرِينَ الَّذِينَ خَسِرُوا أَنفُسَهُمْ وَأَهْلِيهِمْ يَوْمَ الْقِيَامَةِ أَلَا ذَٰلِكَ هُوَ الْخُسْرَانُ الْمُبِينُ

So you (all) worship whatever you want (false gods) from besides Him (Allah), say (O prophet Muhammad, peace be upon him; surely, the losers are those who lost nafs (selves) of theirs and families of theirs, on the day of resurrection (day of judgment), beware, that (loss), it is the loss clear (open and obvious)

Aya 39:16

لَهُم مِّن فَوْقِهِمْ ظُلَلٌ مِّنَ النَّارِ وَمِن تَحْتِهِمْ ظُلَلٌ ذَٰلِكَ يُخَوِّفُ اللَّهُ بِهِ عِبَادَهُ يَا عِبَادِ فَاتَّقُونِ

For them (those losers disbelievers) will be from above them, coverings (layers of fire, overshadowing) from the fire and from underneath them, coverings (layers of fire), that (fire) is, scares (frightens) Allah with it (the fire) servants of His (Allah), O servants of Mine, so fear Me (Allah and practice Taqwa for the sake of Me)

Aya 39:17

وَالَّذِينَ اجْتَنَبُوا الطَّاغُوتَ أَن يَعْبُدُوهَا وَأَنَابُوا إِلَى اللَّهِ لَهُمُ الْبُشْرَىٰ فَبَشِّرْ عِبَادِ

And those (people) who avoided (stayed away from) the Taaghoot (false gods, shaitaan, forces of rebellion against Allah), that they (avoided) to worship it (the Taaghoot) and they turned (in worship and repentance) toward (One) Allah, for them (avoiders of Taaghoot) is the good news (of good life in this world and paradise in the hereafter), so give the good news (O prophet Muhammad peace be upon him) to servants of Mine (Allah)

Aya 39:18

الَّذِينَ يَسْتَمِعُونَ الْقَوْلَ فَيَتَّبِعُونَ أَحْسَنَهُ أُولَٰئِكَ الَّذِينَ هَدَاهُمُ اللَّهُ وَأُولَٰئِكَ هُمْ أُولُو الْأَلْبَابِ

Those (servants of Mine-Allah) who listen to the saying (speech, word, narrative), so they follow (obey) the best of it (of that speech), those are (the people) who guided them Allah, and those are (the people) who are owners of the wit (intelligence, understanding)

Aya 39:19

أَفَمَنْ حَقَّ عَلَيْهِ كَلِمَةُ الْعَذَابِ أَفَأَنتَ تُنقِذُ مَن فِي النَّارِ

So, is the one (person that) came true (got established) on (against) him word (decree) of the punishment (from Allah), so are you (O prophet Muhammad, peace be upon him) to rescue (save) the one who is in the fire?

Aya 39:20

لَٰكِنِ الَّذِينَ اتَّقَوْا رَبَّهُمْ لَهُمْ غُرَفٌ مِّن فَوْقِهَا غُرَفٌ مَّبْنِيَّةٌ تَجْرِي مِن تَحْتِهَا الْأَنْهَارُ وَعْدَ اللَّهِ لَا يُخْلِفُ اللَّهُ الْمِيعَادَ

But those (people) who feared (practiced Taqwa by avoiding sins for fear of Allah) Lord of theirs (Allah), for them are rooms (chambers, places of residence) from above it, are rooms built (ready to be used), flowing from underneath it (rooms) are rivers, (a) promise of Allah, does not oppose (break, fail) Allah the promise

Aya 39:21

أَلَمْ تَرَ أَنَّ اللَّهَ أَنزَلَ مِنَ السَّمَاءِ مَاءً فَسَلَكَهُ يَنَابِيعَ فِي الْأَرْضِ ثُمَّ يُخْرِجُ بِهِ زَرْعًا مُّخْتَلِفًا أَلْوَانُهُ ثُمَّ يَهِيجُ فَتَرَاهُ مُصْفَرًّا ثُمَّ يَجْعَلُهُ حُطَامًا إِنَّ فِي ذَٰلِكَ لَذِكْرَىٰ لِأُولِي الْأَلْبَابِ

Have not you seen that Allah sent down from the sky (heaven) water? So, He (Allah) gave way (path) to it (to the water) as fountains (springs) in the earth, then He (Allah) brings out on it (with water) plants, different are colors of it (of plants), then it becomes dry, so you see it (those plants) turned yellow, then He (Allah) makes it (those plants as) debris, surely in that (process), definitely, is remembrance (reminder) for the owners of wit (people with intelligence and understanding)

Aya 39:22

أَفَمَن شَرَحَ اللَّهُ صَدْرَهُ لِلْإِسْلَامِ فَهُوَ عَلَىٰ نُورٍ مِّن رَّبِّهِ فَوَيْلٌ لِّلْقَاسِيَةِ قُلُوبُهُم مِّن ذِكْرِ اللَّهِ أُولَٰئِكَ فِي ضَلَالٍ مُّبِينٍ

So, is the one, expanded (opened) Allah, chest (heart) of his, for Islam (submission to Allah), so he is on the light (guidance) from Lord of his (Allah, is that true believer equal to a disbeliever)? So destruction (woe) is for hardeners of hearts of theirs from the remembrance of Allah, those (who harden their heart from the remembrance of Allah) are in misguidance (error) open (clear, manifest)

Aya 39:23

اللَّهُ نَزَّلَ أَحْسَنَ الْحَدِيثِ كِتَابًا مُّتَشَابِهًا مَّثَانِيَ تَقْشَعِرُّ مِنْهُ جُلُودُ الَّذِينَ يَخْشَوْنَ رَبَّهُمْ ثُمَّ تَلِينُ جُلُودُهُمْ وَقُلُوبُهُمْ إِلَىٰ ذِكْرِ اللَّهِ ذَٰلِكَ هُدَى اللَّهِ يَهْدِي بِهِ مَن يَشَاءُ وَمَن يُضْلِلِ اللَّهُ فَمَا لَهُ مِنْ هَادٍ

Allah has sent down (revealed) best of the speech (statement, talk), a book (Quran), similar (parts of Quran similar to each other, supporting and reinforcing in a similar fashion), doubling (repeating same subjects over and over), goosebumps (shivers, quivers) from it (reading of Quran) skins of those, (who) fear Lord of theirs (Allah), then soften skins of theirs and hearts of theirs toward remembrance of Allah, that is (the) guidance of Allah, He (Allah) guides on (with) it (with Quran) the one He (Allah) wants (wills), and the one (who) misguides him, Allah, so not is there for him (for that misguided person) from any guider (any one that will guide him after Allah)

Aya 39:24

أَفَمَن يَتَّقِي بِوَجْهِهِ سُوءَ الْعَذَابِ يَوْمَ الْقِيَامَةِ وَقِيلَ لِلظَّالِمِينَ ذُوقُوا مَا كُنتُمْ تَكْسِبُونَ

So, is the one who protects (shields, avoids) on (with) face of his, worst of the punishment, on the day of resurrection (day of judgment, is equal to residents of paradise)?, and (will be) said to the oppressors (unjust people), taste (the punishment of bad deeds) what you were earning (doing injustice in the worldly life)

Aya 39:25

كَذَّبَ الَّذِينَ مِن قَبْلِهِمْ فَأَتَاهُمُ الْعَذَابُ مِنْ حَيْثُ لَا يَشْعُرُونَ

Belied (rejected as a lie) those (people) from before them, so came to them the punishment (of Allah) from where not were they comprehending (understanding)

Aya 39:26

فَأَذَاقَهُمُ اللَّهُ الْخِزْيَ فِي الْحَيَاةِ الدُّنْيَا ۖ وَلَعَذَابُ الْآخِرَةِ أَكْبَرُ ۚ لَوْ كَانُوا يَعْلَمُونَ

So, made them taste Allah, the humiliation (disgrace) in the life of the world and definitely, the punishment of the hereafter is bigger (is worse) if they were knowing

Aya 39:27

وَلَقَدْ ضَرَبْنَا لِلنَّاسِ فِي هَٰذَا الْقُرْآنِ مِن كُلِّ مَثَلٍ لَّعَلَّهُمْ يَتَذَكَّرُونَ

And surely, We (Allah) struck (described, explained), for the people in this Quran from every (all) example (parable, similitude), perhaps they (people) take remembrance (will be reminded, will learn a lesson)

Aya 39:28

قُرْآنًا عَرَبِيًّا غَيْرَ ذِي عِوَجٍ لَّعَلَّهُمْ يَتَّقُونَ

Quran Arabic, not with any crookedness (without any fault, without any deviation from the truth), perhaps they (people) will practice Taqwa (avoiding sins for fear of Allah)

Aya 39:29

ضَرَبَ اللَّهُ مَثَلًا رَّجُلًا فِيهِ شُرَكَاءُ مُتَشَاكِسُونَ وَرَجُلًا سَلَمًا لِّرَجُلٍ هَلْ يَسْتَوِيَانِ مَثَلًا ۚ الْحَمْدُ لِلَّهِ ۚ بَلْ أَكْثَرُهُمْ لَا يَعْلَمُونَ

Struck (described) Allah, an example (parable, similitude), a man in him are partners quarrelsome (opposing, conflicting) and a man wholly (totally) for a man, are the two (men) equal for example? The praise (all of it) is (only) for Allah, but (no, no, rather) most of them (people), not they know (have no knowledge)

Aya 39:30

إِنَّكَ مَيِّتٌ وَإِنَّهُم مَّيِّتُونَ

Surely you (O prophet Muhammad, peace be upon him) are (to be) dead, and they (disbelievers) are (to be) dead.
(Everyone will die)

Aya 39:31

ثُمَّ إِنَّكُمْ يَوْمَ الْقِيَامَةِ عِندَ رَبِّكُمْ تَخْتَصِمُونَ

Then, surely you (all), on the day of resurrection (day of judgment), with Lord of yours (Allah), you will be arguing (disputing)

Aya 39:32

فَمَنْ أَظْلَمُ مِمَّن كَذَبَ عَلَى اللَّهِ وَكَذَّبَ بِالصِّدْقِ إِذْ جَاءَهُ أَلَيْسَ فِي جَهَنَّمَ مَثْوًى لِّلْكَافِرِينَ

So, who is more oppressor (more unjust) from (as compared to the one) who belied (rejected as a lie) on Allah and he belied (rejected) on the truth (Quran) when it (the truth) came (reached) to him? Is there not in the hellfire place of living for the disbelievers (rejectors of the truth)?

Aya 39:33

وَالَّذِي جَاءَ بِالصِّدْقِ وَصَدَّقَ بِهِ أُولَٰئِكَ هُمُ الْمُتَّقُونَ

And the one (prophet Muhammad, peace be upon him) who came on (with) the truth (Quran) and (the one who) confirmed on it (accepted Quran as the truth), those (people), they are the pious (people with Taqwa, avoiding sins for fear of Allah)

Aya 39:34

لَهُم مَّا يَشَاءُونَ عِندَ رَبِّهِمْ ذَٰلِكَ جَزَاءُ الْمُحْسِنِينَ

For them (for truly pious people), is what they want, with the Lord of theirs (Allah), that is the reward of the good doers.

Aya 39:35

لِيُكَفِّرَ اللَّهُ عَنْهُمْ أَسْوَأَ الَّذِي عَمِلُوا وَيَجْزِيَهُمْ أَجْرَهُم بِأَحْسَنِ الَّذِي كَانُوا يَعْمَلُونَ

For to remove (erase) Allah from them (righteous people) the worst of what they did (sins of theirs) and He (Allah) reward them, the reward of theirs, on the best of what they were doing (in the worldly life)

Aya 39:36

أَلَيْسَ اللَّهُ بِكَافٍ عَبْدَهُ وَيُخَوِّفُونَكَ بِالَّذِينَ مِن دُونِهِ وَمَن يُضْلِلِ اللَّهُ فَمَا لَهُ مِنْ هَادٍ

Is not Allah sufficient for the servant of His (servant of Allah, meaning prophet Mohammad, peace be upon him, to protect him from harm)? And they (disbelievers) scare (frighten you, with harm for) you ((O prophet Muhammad peace be upon him) on (with) those (harm from false gods) beside Him (Allah) and whomever misguides Allah (put him astray), so not is there for him from any guider (guiding authority other than Allah)

Aya 39:37

وَمَن يَهْدِ اللَّهُ فَمَا لَهُ مِن مُّضِلٍّ أَلَيْسَ اللَّهُ بِعَزِيزٍ ذِي انتِقَامٍ

And the one Allah guides, so not is there for him, from any misleader (to misguide him and put him on the wrong path), is not Allah the All-Mighty Owner of the revenge (retaliation)

Aya 39:38

وَلَئِن سَأَلْتَهُم مَّنْ خَلَقَ السَّمَاوَاتِ وَالْأَرْضَ لَيَقُولُنَّ اللَّهُ قُلْ أَفَرَأَيْتُم مَّا تَدْعُونَ مِن دُونِ اللَّهِ إِنْ أَرَادَنِيَ اللَّهُ بِضُرٍّ هَلْ هُنَّ كَاشِفَاتُ ضُرِّهِ أَوْ أَرَادَنِي بِرَحْمَةٍ هَلْ هُنَّ مُمْسِكَاتُ رَحْمَتِهِ قُلْ حَسْبِيَ اللَّهُ عَلَيْهِ يَتَوَكَّلُ الْمُتَوَكِّلُونَ

And if you asked them (disbelievers), who created the skies (heavens) and the earth?, definitely, they (disbelievers) will say, Allah (is the Creator), say (O prophet Muhammad peace be upon him) so did you see (considered, thought) what (false gods) you are calling (invoking and worshiping) from besides Allah, if intended for me Allah, on any harm, are they (your false gods) removers of the harm of His (Allah), or if He (Allah) intended for me, on mercy, are they (your false gods) withholders (stopper) of the mercy of His (Allah)?, say (O prophet Muhammad peace be upon him) enough (sufficient) for me is Allah (against any perceived harm by your false gods), on Him (only on Allah) trust (rely and depend) the (true) trustors

Aya 39:39

قُلْ يَا قَوْمِ اعْمَلُوا عَلَىٰ مَكَانَتِكُمْ إِنِّي عَامِلٌ فَسَوْفَ تَعْلَمُونَ

Say (O prophet Muhammad, peace be upon him), "O nation (people) of mine, you do (act) on place (position, status) of yours (you do what you do), surely, I, am doer (on my place or position, I do what I do), so soon you will know (the result)

Aya 39:40
مَن يَأْتِيهِ عَذَابٌ يُخْزِيهِ وَيَحِلُّ عَلَيْهِ عَذَابٌ مُّقِيمٌ

(Soon you will know), Who is the one that comes to him punishment that humiliates him and (who is the one, that) becomes due (descends, befalls) on him punishment stayer (continuing or everlasting)

Aya 39:41
إِنَّا أَنزَلْنَا عَلَيْكَ الْكِتَابَ لِلنَّاسِ بِالْحَقِّ فَمَنِ اهْتَدَىٰ فَلِنَفْسِهِ وَمَن ضَلَّ فَإِنَّمَا يَضِلُّ عَلَيْهَا وَمَا أَنتَ عَلَيْهِم بِوَكِيلٍ

Surely, We (Allah), We sent down (revealed), on you, the book (Quran), for people on truth, so the one who took the guidance, so (the benefit of that guidance) is for self (nafs, person) of his and the one who took misguidance, so surely that he misguides on it (on self of his, punishment of misguidance is against himself) and not are you (O prophet Muhammad peace be upon him) on them (these people) guardian (take-carer, responsible, manager, custodian)

Aya 39:42
اللَّهُ يَتَوَفَّى الْأَنفُسَ حِينَ مَوْتِهَا وَالَّتِي لَمْ تَمُتْ فِي مَنَامِهَا فَيُمْسِكُ الَّتِي قَضَىٰ عَلَيْهَا الْمَوْتَ وَيُرْسِلُ الْأُخْرَىٰ إِلَىٰ أَجَلٍ مُّسَمًّى إِنَّ فِي ذَٰلِكَ لَآيَاتٍ لِّقَوْمٍ يَتَفَكَّرُونَ

Allah makes to die, the selves (nafs, persons) at the time of death of it (of that person) and the one (nafs) not died, (is taken away) in sleep of it (nafs), so He (Allah) withholds (stop, prevents from coming back) the one decided on it (on that nafs or person) the death and He (Allah) sends (back) the others (the one not decided death of it, to stay alive) till appointed time, named (already known), surely in that, definitely are signs for nation (people) who think (reflect and ponder)

Aya 39:43
أَمِ اتَّخَذُوا مِن دُونِ اللَّهِ شُفَعَاءَ قُلْ أَوَلَوْ كَانُوا لَا يَمْلِكُونَ شَيْئًا وَلَا يَعْقِلُونَ

Or have they made (taken) from besides Allah intercessors (false gods to intercede and save them from the punishment of Allah)? Say (O prophet Muhammad, peace be upon him), even if they (those false intercessors) are not owning (possessing) anything (any power) and not are they (those false presumed intercessor gods) having intelligence (understanding)?

Aya 39:44

قُل لِّلَّهِ الشَّفَاعَةُ جَمِيعًا ۖ لَّهُ مُلْكُ السَّمَاوَاتِ وَالْأَرْضِ ۖ ثُمَّ إِلَيْهِ تُرْجَعُونَ

Say (O prophet Muhammad, peace be upon him), (only) for Allah is the intercession, all of it, for Him (Allah) is the kingdom of the skies (heavens) and the earth, then toward Him (Allah) you (all) will be returned.

Aya 39:45

وَإِذَا ذُكِرَ اللَّهُ وَحْدَهُ اشْمَأَزَّتْ قُلُوبُ الَّذِينَ لَا يُؤْمِنُونَ بِالْآخِرَةِ ۖ وَإِذَا ذُكِرَ الَّذِينَ مِن دُونِهِ إِذَا هُمْ يَسْتَبْشِرُونَ

And when is remembered (mentioned) Allah alone, shrink (with disgust) hearts of those (people) who are not believing on the hereafter and when are mentioned those (false gods) from beside Him (Allah), then they (disbelievers) are rejoicing (taking glad tidings, are happy)

Aya 39:46

قُلِ اللَّهُمَّ فَاطِرَ السَّمَاوَاتِ وَالْأَرْضِ عَالِمَ الْغَيْبِ وَالشَّهَادَةِ أَنتَ تَحْكُمُ بَيْنَ عِبَادِكَ فِي مَا كَانُوا فِيهِ يَخْتَلِفُونَ

Say (O prophet Muhammad, peace be upon him), O Allah, Originator of the skies (heavens) and the earth, Knower of the unseen and the witnessed (evident), You (Allah) will decide (judge) in between servants of Yours in what they (Your servants) were, in it, differing

Aya 39:47

وَلَوْ أَنَّ لِلَّذِينَ ظَلَمُوا مَا فِي الْأَرْضِ جَمِيعًا وَمِثْلَهُ مَعَهُ لَافْتَدَوْا بِهِ مِن سُوءِ الْعَذَابِ يَوْمَ الْقِيَامَةِ ۚ وَبَدَا لَهُم مِّنَ اللَّهِ مَا لَمْ يَكُونُوا يَحْتَسِبُونَ

And if that, for those who oppressed (others or acted unjustly) had (the ownership of) whatever is in the earth, all of it and like it with it, definitely, they would give ransom (compensation) on it, (of all their wealth, to get saved) from the bad of the punishment, on the day of resurrection (judgment) and became evident (clear) for them, from Allah, what they were not supposing (thinking, expecting)

Aya 39:48

وَبَدَا لَهُمْ سَيِّئَاتُ مَا كَسَبُوا وَحَاقَ بِهِم مَّا كَانُوا بِهِ يَسْتَهْزِئُونَ

And became evident (clear) for them bad deeds, what they earned (did in worldly life) and encircled (enveloped, befell) on them what (punishment of Allah) they were on it (on the punishment of Allah) joking (ridiculing, mocking)

Aya 39:49

فَإِذَا مَسَّ الْإِنسَانَ ضُرٌّ دَعَانَا ثُمَّ إِذَا خَوَّلْنَاهُ نِعْمَةً مِّنَّا قَالَ إِنَّمَا أُوتِيتُهُ عَلَىٰ عِلْمٍ ۚ بَلْ هِيَ فِتْنَةٌ وَلَٰكِنَّ أَكْثَرَهُمْ لَا يَعْلَمُونَ

So when touches the human (any) harm (hurt, adversity), he called (invoked, prayed to) Us (Allah), then when We (Allah) bestowed (gave) him (the human) a giving (favor, grace) from Us (from Allah- a giving and a gift from Allah), he (human) said, surely, what was given to me, it (this favor or giving) is on (due to my) knowledge, but (no, no, rather) it (this saying, I was given due to my knowledge) is a testing (trial), but most of them, not they know

Aya 39:50

قَدْ قَالَهَا الَّذِينَ مِن قَبْلِهِمْ فَمَا أَغْنَىٰ عَنْهُم مَّا كَانُوا يَكْسِبُونَ

Surely, said it (this saying, I was given, due to my knowledge) those (people) from before them, so not saved (benefited) from them (from the punishment of Allah) what they were earning (doing)

Aya 39:51

فَأَصَابَهُمْ سَيِّئَاتُ مَا كَسَبُوا ۚ وَالَّذِينَ ظَلَمُوا مِنْ هَٰؤُلَاءِ سَيُصِيبُهُمْ سَيِّئَاتُ مَا كَسَبُوا وَمَا هُم بِمُعْجِزِينَ

So reached them (befell on those earlier people that were saying, I was given due to my knowledge), evils (bad consequences) of what they earned (did) and those who oppressed (others, acted unjustly) from these (current people), soon will reach them (befall on them) evils (bad consequences) of what they earned (did) and not are they frustrators (to overcome or defeat Allah and escape the punishment of Allah)

Aya 39:52

أَوَلَمْ يَعْلَمُوا أَنَّ اللَّهَ يَبْسُطُ الرِّزْقَ لِمَن يَشَاءُ وَيَقْدِرُ ۚ إِنَّ فِي ذَٰلِكَ لَآيَاتٍ لِّقَوْمٍ يُؤْمِنُونَ

Do not they (disbelievers) know that Allah spreads (expands, increases) the sustenance (food and wealth) for the one He (Allah) wants (wills) and measures (restricts or decreases food and wealth for some)? Surely, in that (increasing and decreasing of sustenance), definitely, are signs for nation (people) they (who) believe

17

Aya 39:53

قُلْ يَا عِبَادِيَ الَّذِينَ أَسْرَفُوا عَلَىٰ أَنفُسِهِمْ لَا تَقْنَطُوا مِن رَّحْمَةِ اللَّهِ إِنَّ اللَّهَ يَغْفِرُ الذُّنُوبَ جَمِيعًا إِنَّهُ هُوَ الْغَفُورُ الرَّحِيمُ

Say (O prophet Muhammad, peace be upon him) O servants of Mine (servants of Allah), those who acted extravagantly (transgressed) on (against) selves (nafs, person) of theirs, not you despair (be hopeless) from the mercy of Allah, surely, Allah forgives the sins, all of it, surely, He (Allah) is the Most Forgiver, The Most Merciful

Aya 39:54

وَأَنِيبُوا إِلَىٰ رَبِّكُمْ وَأَسْلِمُوا لَهُ مِن قَبْلِ أَن يَأْتِيَكُمُ الْعَذَابُ ثُمَّ لَا تُنصَرُونَ

And return (turn back in repentance) toward Lord of yours (Allah) and submit (be obedient) for Him (Allah), from before that comes to you the punishment (of Allah), then not will you be helped (after coming of the punishment)

Aya 39:55

وَاتَّبِعُوا أَحْسَنَ مَا أُنزِلَ إِلَيْكُم مِّن رَّبِّكُم مِّن قَبْلِ أَن يَأْتِيَكُمُ الْعَذَابُ بَغْتَةً وَأَنتُمْ لَا تَشْعُرُونَ

And obey (follow) the best (Quran), what was sent down (revealed) toward you, from Lord of yours (Allah), from before that comes to you the punishment (of Allah) suddenly and (while) not you comprehend (understand)

Aya 39:56

أَن تَقُولَ نَفْسٌ يَا حَسْرَتَا عَلَىٰ مَا فَرَّطتُ فِي جَنبِ اللَّهِ وَإِن كُنتُ لَمِنَ السَّاخِرِينَ

(Follow the Quran before the punishment comes otherwise) That may say a nafs (self, a person), O alas (regret, pity) on me, on (that) I fell short (neglected) in the side of Allah (in obeying Allah), and surely I was, definitely, from the mockers (making fun of Islam)

Aya 39:57

أَوْ تَقُولَ لَوْ أَنَّ اللَّهَ هَدَانِي لَكُنتُ مِنَ الْمُتَّقِينَ

Or may say (the nafs, a person), if surely, that Allah had guided me, definitely, I would have been from the pious (people, who avoid sins for the fear of Allah)

Aya 39:58

أَوْ تَقُولَ حِينَ تَرَى الْعَذَابَ لَوْ أَنَّ لِي كَرَّةً فَأَكُونَ مِنَ الْمُحْسِنِينَ

Or may say (the nafs, a person) when it sees the punishment (of Allah) if surely that, for me, was (another) turn (another chance) so I will become from the good-doers.

Aya 39:59

بَلَىٰ قَدْ جَاءَتْكَ آيَاتِي فَكَذَّبْتَ بِهَا وَاسْتَكْبَرْتَ وَكُنتَ مِنَ الْكَافِرِينَ

Yes, surely, came to you, signs (verses) of Mine (verses of Allah), so you belied (rejected) on it (on signs of Allah) and you practiced arrogance (with signs of Allah) and you were from the disbelievers (rejectors)

Aya 39:60

وَيَوْمَ الْقِيَامَةِ تَرَى الَّذِينَ كَذَبُوا عَلَى اللَّهِ وُجُوهُهُم مُّسْوَدَّةٌ أَلَيْسَ فِي جَهَنَّمَ مَثْوًى لِّلْمُتَكَبِّرِينَ

And on the day of resurrection, you will see those who lied on (against) Allah (false attributions to Allah), faces of theirs (will be) blackened, is not there in the hell place of living for arrogant (people)?

Aya 39:61

وَيُنَجِّي اللَّهُ الَّذِينَ اتَّقَوْا بِمَفَازَتِهِمْ لَا يَمَسُّهُمُ السُّوءُ وَلَا هُمْ يَحْزَنُونَ

And will save Allah (from hellfire), those who feared Allah (who practiced taqwa-avoiding sins for the fear of Allah) on (places of) success of theirs (paradise), not will touch them the harm (hurt) and not will they sadden (will not be sad and unhappy)

Aya 39:62

اللَّهُ خَالِقُ كُلِّ شَيْءٍ وَهُوَ عَلَىٰ كُلِّ شَيْءٍ وَكِيلٌ

Allah is the Creator of all things, and He (Allah) is on all things Take-Carer (Guardian, Trustee).

Aya 39:63

لَّهُ مَقَالِيدُ السَّمَاوَاتِ وَالْأَرْضِ وَالَّذِينَ كَفَرُوا بِآيَاتِ اللَّهِ أُولَٰئِكَ هُمُ الْخَاسِرُونَ

(Only) for Him (Allah) are keys (to treasures) of the skies (heavens) and the earth, and those who disbelieved (rejected) on signs (verses) of Allah, those, they are the losers.

Aya 39:64

قُلْ أَفَغَيْرَ اللَّهِ تَأْمُرُونِّي أَعْبُدُ أَيُّهَا الْجَاهِلُونَ

Say (O prophet Muhammad, peace be upon him), so, is it (that) other than Allah, you are ordering (commanding) me, (that) I worship O (you) the ignorant (people)?

Aya 39:65

وَلَقَدْ أُوحِيَ إِلَيْكَ وَإِلَى الَّذِينَ مِن قَبْلِكَ لَئِنْ أَشْرَكْتَ لَيَحْبَطَنَّ عَمَلُكَ وَلَتَكُونَنَّ مِنَ الْخَاسِرِينَ

And surely, it is revealed (from Allah) toward you and toward those (people) from before you, if you made partners (with Allah), definitely, nullified (useless) will become deeds of yours, and definitely, you will become from the losers

Aya 39:66

بَلِ اللَّهَ فَاعْبُدْ وَكُن مِّنَ الشَّاكِرِينَ

But (no, no rather), (only One) Allah, so you (must) worship and be from the grateful (people who are thankful to Allah)

Aya 39:67

وَمَا قَدَرُوا اللَّهَ حَقَّ قَدْرِهِ وَالْأَرْضُ جَمِيعًا قَبْضَتُهُ يَوْمَ الْقِيَامَةِ وَالسَّمَاوَاتُ مَطْوِيَّاتٌ بِيَمِينِهِ سُبْحَانَهُ وَتَعَالَىٰ عَمَّا يُشْرِكُونَ

And not, they (disbelievers and polytheists) honored (respected, valued) Allah the true honor (respect) of Him (by associating partners with Allah) and the earth, all (of it, whole of it) is in grip (grasp, control) of His (Allah), on the day of resurrection and skies (heavens) rolled up (folded) on the right hand of His (Allah), purity (glory) is to Him (Allah) and supremely High (exalted and much above) is He (Allah) from what (false gods), they (disbelievers) are making partners (with Allah)

Aya 39:68

وَنُفِخَ فِي الصُّورِ فَصَعِقَ مَن فِي السَّمَاوَاتِ وَمَن فِي الْأَرْضِ إِلَّا مَن شَاءَ اللَّهُ ثُمَّ نُفِخَ فِيهِ أُخْرَىٰ فَإِذَا هُمْ قِيَامٌ يَنظُرُونَ

And (on the day of resurrection) blown into the trumpet,
so fainted (stunned to death) the ones (all those) in the skies (heavens) and the ones (all those) in the earth except the ones willed (wanted) Allah (those will stay alive), then blown into it (trumpet) another (time), so then (after the 2nd trumpet), they are standing looking (on or waiting)

Aya 39:69

وَأَشْرَقَتِ الْأَرْضُ بِنُورِ رَبِّهَا وَوُضِعَ الْكِتَابُ وَجِيءَ بِالنَّبِيِّينَ وَالشُّهَدَاءِ وَقُضِيَ بَيْنَهُم بِالْحَقِّ وَهُمْ لَا يُظْلَمُونَ

And got illuminated (lightened, shined) the earth on the light of Lord of it (Allah) and got placed (upfront) the book (of deeds) and were brought (in) the prophets (peace be upon all of them) and the witnesses and got decided in between them on the truth and they, not will they be oppressed (treated unjustly)

Aya 39:70

وَوُفِّيَتْ كُلُّ نَفْسٍ مَّا عَمِلَتْ وَهُوَ أَعْلَمُ بِمَا يَفْعَلُونَ

And was fully given to every nafs (person, reward of) what it did (in the worldly life), and He (Allah) is the Best Knower on what they were doing.

Aya 39:71

وَسِيقَ الَّذِينَ كَفَرُوا إِلَىٰ جَهَنَّمَ زُمَرًا ۖ حَتَّىٰ إِذَا جَاءُوهَا فُتِحَتْ أَبْوَابُهَا وَقَالَ لَهُمْ خَزَنَتُهَا أَلَمْ يَأْتِكُمْ رُسُلٌ مِّنكُمْ يَتْلُونَ عَلَيْكُمْ آيَاتِ رَبِّكُمْ وَيُنذِرُونَكُمْ لِقَاءَ يَوْمِكُمْ هَٰذَا ۚ قَالُوا بَلَىٰ وَلَٰكِنْ حَقَّتْ كَلِمَةُ الْعَذَابِ عَلَى الْكَافِرِينَ

And driven will be, those who disbelieved (rejected the message of Islam in the worldly life) toward hellfire in groups, till they came to it (hellfire), were opened doors of it (of hell) and said for them, keepers (guards) of it (of hell), did not come to you messengers (peace be upon all of them) from (amongst) you, they reciting on you signs (verses) of Lord of yours (Allah) and warning (scaring) you, the meeting of the day of yours, this one? They (disbelievers) said, yes, but became true (due) the word of punishment on the disbelievers.

Aya 39:72

قِيلَ ادْخُلُوا أَبْوَابَ جَهَنَّمَ خَالِدِينَ فِيهَا ۖ فَبِئْسَ مَثْوَى الْمُتَكَبِّرِينَ

Was said (to disbelievers), enter doors of hell, stayers (living) forever in it (hell), so bad is (the) place of living of the arrogant (disbelievers)

Aya 39:73

وَسِيقَ الَّذِينَ اتَّقَوْا رَبَّهُمْ إِلَى الْجَنَّةِ زُمَرًا ۖ حَتَّىٰ إِذَا جَاءُوهَا وَفُتِحَتْ أَبْوَابُهَا وَقَالَ لَهُمْ خَزَنَتُهَا سَلَامٌ عَلَيْكُمْ طِبْتُمْ فَادْخُلُوهَا خَالِدِينَ

And driven were those who feared Lord of theirs (practiced Taqwa-avoided sins for the fear of Allah) toward the Garden (paradise) in groups, till when they came to it (paradise) and were opened doors of it (paradise) and said for them keepers (guards) of it (paradise), salaam (peace) be on you (all), you did well, so enter it (paradise) stayers forever (living in there forever)

Aya 39:74

وَقَالُوا الْحَمْدُ لِلَّهِ الَّذِي صَدَقَنَا وَعْدَهُ وَأَوْرَثَنَا الْأَرْضَ نَتَبَوَّأُ مِنَ الْجَنَّةِ حَيْثُ نَشَاءُ فَنِعْمَ أَجْرُ الْعَامِلِينَ

And they (residents of paradise) said, (all) praise is for Allah, the One (Allah) Who made true with us promise of His (Allah) and He made us inherit the earth (land), we make the place (of living) from the Garden (paradise), where we want, so excellent is the reward of the doers (doers of good deeds)

Aya 39:75

وَتَرَى الْمَلَائِكَةَ حَافِّينَ مِنْ حَوْلِ الْعَرْشِ يُسَبِّحُونَ بِحَمْدِ رَبِّهِمْ وَقُضِيَ بَيْنَهُمْ بِالْحَقِّ وَقِيلَ الْحَمْدُ لِلَّهِ رَبِّ الْعَالَمِينَ

And you will see the angels, encircling from around the Arsh (the throne of Allah) proclaiming purity (glorifying) on praise of Lord of theirs (Allah) and got decided in between them (all people, all disputes they had in the worldly life) on truth (justice) and was said, (all) the praise is for Allah, Lord of the universes.

سورة غافر

Surah Ghaafir

The Glorious Quran 40

بِسْمِ اللَّهِ الرَّحْمَٰنِ الرَّحِيمِ

(I begin) with the name of Allah, the Most Kind (beneficent), the Most Merciful

Aya 40:1

حم

Haa Meem

Only Allah knows the meaning of these alphabets (called Huroof e Muqatta'at)

Aya 40:2

تَنزِيلُ الْكِتَابِ مِنَ اللَّهِ الْعَزِيزِ الْعَلِيمِ

Revelation of the Book (Quran) is from Allah, the All-Mighty, the All-Knower

Aya 40:3

غَافِرِ الذَّنبِ وَقَابِلِ التَّوْبِ شَدِيدِ الْعِقَابِ ذِي الطَّوْلِ لَا إِلَٰهَ إِلَّا هُوَ إِلَيْهِ الْمَصِيرُ

(Allah) The Forgiver of the sin, the Acceptor of the repentance, the Intense in (giving) the punishment, the Owner of the capacity (Owner of the power, plenty of bounties, abundance), none (anyone) is worthy of worship except He (Allah), toward Him (Allah), is the (final) return

Aya 40:4

مَا يُجَادِلُ فِي آيَاتِ اللَّهِ إِلَّا الَّذِينَ كَفَرُوا فَلَا يَغْرُرْكَ تَقَلُّبُهُمْ فِي الْبِلَادِ

Not quarrel (dispute) in signs (verses of Quran) of Allah except those (people who) rejected (disbelieved Quran), so not to deceive (trick) you, moving around (as prosperous people) of theirs (disbelievers) in towns (cities, lands)

Aya 40:5

كَذَّبَتْ قَبْلَهُمْ قَوْمُ نُوحٍ وَالْأَحْزَابُ مِن بَعْدِهِمْ وَهَمَّتْ كُلُّ أُمَّةٍ بِرَسُولِهِمْ لِيَأْخُذُوهُ وَجَادَلُوا بِالْبَاطِلِ لِيُدْحِضُوا بِهِ الْحَقَّ فَأَخَذْتُهُمْ فَكَيْفَ كَانَ عِقَابِ

Belied (rejected) before them (current disbelievers), the nation (people) of (prophet) Nuh (peace be upon him) and the (many) groups (nations) from after them, and tried (made a plot against, seized, attacked) every nation on (against) messenger (peace be upon all of them) of theirs, to get hold of (seize) him (the messenger peace be upon him) and they fought on (with the help of) falsehood, to refute (invalidate, rebut) on (with) it (with falsehood) the truth, so I held (seized and punished those nations) so how (severe) was the punishment of Mine (of Allah)

Aya 40:6

وَكَذَٰلِكَ حَقَّتْ كَلِمَتُ رَبِّكَ عَلَى الَّذِينَ كَفَرُوا أَنَّهُمْ أَصْحَابُ النَّارِ

And like that, became true (became due) the word of (punishment from) Lord of yours (Allah), on those (against those people who) rejected (disbelieved), that they are companions of fire.

Aya 40:7

الَّذِينَ يَحْمِلُونَ الْعَرْشَ وَمَنْ حَوْلَهُ يُسَبِّحُونَ بِحَمْدِ رَبِّهِمْ وَيُؤْمِنُونَ بِهِ وَيَسْتَغْفِرُونَ لِلَّذِينَ آمَنُوا رَبَّنَا وَسِعْتَ كُلَّ شَيْءٍ رَّحْمَةً وَعِلْمًا فَاغْفِرْ لِلَّذِينَ تَابُوا وَاتَّبَعُوا سَبِيلَكَ وَقِهِمْ عَذَابَ الْجَحِيمِ

Those (angels who) are carrying (bearing) the Arsh (throne of Allah) and those (angels who are) around it (the Arsh), they (those angels) are proclaiming purity on (with) praise of Lord of theirs (Allah) and they are believing on Him (Allah), and they (those angels) are asking (Allah's) forgiveness for those (people who) believed (in Allah and his religion), (those angels praying) O Lord of ours (Allah), you expanded (encompassed, surrounded) every (all) things in mercy and knowledge, so forgive for those (people who) repented (from sins for the sake of Allah) and followed path of Yours (path of Allah) and protect them (those true believers) from the punishment of the hell.

Aya 40:8

رَبَّنَا وَأَدْخِلْهُمْ جَنَّاتِ عَدْنٍ الَّتِي وَعَدتَّهُمْ وَمَن صَلَحَ مِنْ آبَائِهِمْ وَأَزْوَاجِهِمْ وَذُرِّيَّاتِهِمْ إِنَّكَ أَنتَ الْعَزِيزُ الْحَكِيمُ

(Those angels praying) O Lord of ours and enter (admit) them (true believers) in gardens of eternity, those (gardens of eternity) that You (Allah) promised them (true believers) and the ones who did good (deeds) from parents of theirs and spouses of theirs and children of theirs, surely you (O Allah), you are the All-Mighty the All-Wise

Aya 40:9

وَقِهِمُ السَّيِّئَاتِ وَمَن تَقِ السَّيِّئَاتِ يَوْمَئِذٍ فَقَدْ رَحِمْتَهُ وَذَٰلِكَ هُوَ الْفَوْزُ الْعَظِيمُ

(Angels praying) and protect them (true believers) from (punishment of) the bad deeds and the one You (Allah) protected from (punishment of) the bad deeds that day (of judgment), so surely you blessed him with mercy, and that (protection from hellfire) is the success, the great (big success)

Aya 40:10

إِنَّ الَّذِينَ كَفَرُوا يُنَادَوْنَ لَمَقْتُ اللَّهِ أَكْبَرُ مِن مَّقْتِكُمْ أَنفُسَكُمْ إِذْ تُدْعَوْنَ إِلَى الْإِيمَانِ فَتَكْفُرُونَ

Surely, those (people who) disbelieved, will be shouted to (called, announced to by angels); "definitely, dislike (hatred, disgust) of Allah is bigger from dislike (hatred, disgust) of yours for selves of yours, when you were called toward the (true) belief (of Islam) so you rejected (the call to true belief in the worldly life)

Aya 40:11

قَالُوا رَبَّنَا أَمَتَّنَا اثْنَتَيْنِ وَأَحْيَيْتَنَا اثْنَتَيْنِ فَاعْتَرَفْنَا بِذُنُوبِنَا فَهَلْ إِلَىٰ خُرُوجٍ مِّن سَبِيلٍ

They (disbelievers) said, Lord of ours (Allah), you gave us death two times (were dead before, brought to life, then were given death and now are resurrected again), and you gave us life two times, so we confessed on sins of ours, so is there toward getting out (from the hellfire) any way (any path)?

Aya 40:12

ذَٰلِكُم بِأَنَّهُ إِذَا دُعِيَ اللَّهُ وَحْدَهُ كَفَرْتُمْ وَإِن يُشْرَكْ بِهِ تُؤْمِنُوا فَالْحُكْمُ لِلَّهِ الْعَلِيِّ الْكَبِيرِ

That (punishment for) you, because of that, when was called (prayed to, invoked) Allah Alone, you rejected (the Oneness of Allah) and if were made partners on (with) Him (Allah) you believed (in partners as false gods), so the (sole power of) decision is for Allah, the Most High, the Most Great.

Aya 40:13

هُوَ الَّذِي يُرِيكُمْ آيَاتِهِ وَيُنَزِّلُ لَكُم مِّنَ السَّمَاءِ رِزْقًا وَمَا يَتَذَكَّرُ إِلَّا مَن يُنِيبُ

He (Allah) is the One (who) shows you signs of His (Allah), and He brings down (sends down) for you from the skies sustenance (food and provisions) and not will take remembrance (lesson, reminder, understanding) except the one (who) turns (to Allah with sincere acceptance and prayers)

Aya 40:14

فَادْعُوا اللَّهَ مُخْلِصِينَ لَهُ الدِّينَ وَلَوْ كَرِهَ الْكَافِرُونَ

So (all of you) call upon (invoke and pray to) Allah, making sincere (pure and devoted only) for Him (for Allah) the Deen (religion, prayers, way of life) even if (this Oneness of Allah) disliked the disbelievers (rejectors)

Aya 40:15

رَفِيعُ الدَّرَجَاتِ ذُو الْعَرْشِ يُلْقِي الرُّوحَ مِنْ أَمْرِهِ عَلَىٰ مَن يَشَاءُ مِنْ عِبَادِهِ لِيُنذِرَ يَوْمَ التَّلَاقِ

(Only Allah is) the raiser of the ranks (elevator of the status for his servants OR Allah is exalted in ranks/status), Owner of the Arsh (throne of Allah), He (Allah) drops the spirit (send revelation by angel Jibrael) from order of His (Allah), on the one He (Allah) wants (wills to make him a prophet) from servants of His (Allah), so that He (Allah or His messenger) will warn (the people) about the day of meeting (day of encounter with Allah, the day of judgment)

Aya 40:16

يَوْمَ هُم بَارِزُونَ لَا يَخْفَىٰ عَلَى اللَّهِ مِنْهُمْ شَيْءٌ لِّمَنِ الْمُلْكُ الْيَوْمَ لِلَّهِ الْوَاحِدِ الْقَهَّارِ

The day (of judgment) they (disbelievers) will be upfront (in the open, coming forth, standing openly in front of Allah), not will be hidden on Allah from (about) them anything, (will be asked) for whom is the kingdom (authority) this day (of judgment)?, (will be answered, the kingdom and authority is only) for Allah the One (Allah), the One with extreme power of punishment

Aya 40:17

الْيَوْمَ تُجْزَىٰ كُلُّ نَفْسٍ بِمَا كَسَبَتْ لَا ظُلْمَ الْيَوْمَ إِنَّ اللَّهَ سَرِيعُ الْحِسَابِ

Today (on the day of judgment), will be rewarded every self (person, nafs) on what he earned (practiced in the worldly life), not will be there any oppression (injustice) today, surely, Allah is quick in taking accounts (of all deeds)

Aya 40:18

وَأَنذِرْهُمْ يَوْمَ الْآزِفَةِ إِذِ الْقُلُوبُ لَدَى الْحَنَاجِرِ كَاظِمِينَ مَا لِلظَّالِمِينَ مِنْ حَمِيمٍ وَلَا شَفِيعٍ يُطَاعُ

And warn them (O prophet Muhammad, peace be upon him about) the day, the near one (day of judgment which is near), when hearts will be close to throats (meaning very hard and difficult day), (disbelievers will be) repressors (of their pain and anguish), not will be there for oppressors (unjust people that day) from any close friend and not any intercessor (intervening authority that will be) obeyed (listened to)

Aya 40:19

يَعْلَمُ خَائِنَةَ الْأَعْيُنِ وَمَا تُخْفِي الصُّدُورُ

He (Allah) knows the corruption (treachery, trick, deception) of the eyes and what (thoughts and plans) are hiding the chests (secret of the hearts)

Aya 40:20

وَاللَّهُ يَقْضِي بِالْحَقِّ وَالَّذِينَ يَدْعُونَ مِن دُونِهِ لَا يَقْضُونَ بِشَيْءٍ إِنَّ اللَّهَ هُوَ السَّمِيعُ الْبَصِيرُ

And Allah judges (decides, gives verdict) on (the basis of) the truth; and those (people who) they (disbelievers) are calling (invoking, worshiping) from besides Him (other than Allah), not are they judging on anything (nothing from truth), surely Allah is the All-Listener, the All-Seer.

Aya 40:21

أَوَلَمْ يَسِيرُوا فِي الْأَرْضِ فَيَنظُرُوا كَيْفَ كَانَ عَاقِبَةُ الَّذِينَ كَانُوا مِن قَبْلِهِمْ كَانُوا هُمْ أَشَدَّ مِنْهُمْ قُوَّةً وَآثَارًا فِي الْأَرْضِ فَأَخَذَهُمُ اللَّهُ بِذُنُوبِهِمْ وَمَا كَانَ لَهُم مِّنَ اللَّهِ مِن وَاقٍ

And, do not they (disbelievers) travel in the earth (land), so they may look (see), how was the end status of those (people who) were from before them (current disbelievers)? They (those past destroyed nations) were more intense from them (as compared to current disbelievers) in power and traces (impressions, signs, impact they left) in the earth, so got hold of (seized) them Allah on (due to) sins of theirs and not was there for them (those past destroyed nations) from (the punishment of) Allah, from any preventer (protector, defender)

Aya 40:22

ذَٰلِكَ بِأَنَّهُمْ كَانَت تَّأْتِيهِمْ رُسُلُهُم بِالْبَيِّنَاتِ فَكَفَرُوا فَأَخَذَهُمُ اللَّهُ إِنَّهُ قَوِيٌّ شَدِيدُ الْعِقَابِ

That (punishment was) because that they (those past destroyed nations) were coming to them messengers (peace be upon all of them) of theirs on clear evidences (open signs), so they rejected (the message with clear signs), so got hold of (seized) them Allah, surely He (Allah) is the Powerful, Intense in the punishment

Aya 40:23

وَلَقَدْ أَرْسَلْنَا مُوسَىٰ بِآيَاتِنَا وَسُلْطَانٍ مُّبِينٍ

And surely, We sent (prophet) Musa (peace be upon him), on (with) signs of Ours and authority (strong argument) clear (open and evident)

Aya 40:24

إِلَىٰ فِرْعَوْنَ وَهَامَانَ وَقَارُونَ فَقَالُوا سَاحِرٌ كَذَّابٌ

(We sent prophet Musa; peace be upon him) Toward Fir'aon (the king of Egypt) and Haamaan (chief lieutenant of Fira'on) and Qaaroon (Korah-the person with huge treasures) so they said, (prophet Musa peace be upon him is) magician, (severe) liar

Aya 40:25

فَلَمَّا جَاءَهُم بِالْحَقِّ مِنْ عِندِنَا قَالُوا اقْتُلُوا أَبْنَاءَ الَّذِينَ آمَنُوا مَعَهُ وَاسْتَحْيُوا نِسَاءَهُمْ وَمَا كَيْدُ الْكَافِرِينَ إِلَّا فِي ضَلَالٍ

So when (prophet Musa, peace be upon him) came (to) them on (with) the truth (true message of Allah with miracles) from side of Ours (Allah), they said, kill sons of those (people who) believed (in Allah) with him (with prophet Musa peace be upon him) and leave alive women of theirs, and not is plot (plan, trick) of disbelievers except in error (in loss, wrong, unjust, destined to fail)

Aya 40:26

وَقَالَ فِرْعَوْنُ ذَرُونِي أَقْتُلْ مُوسَىٰ وَلْيَدْعُ رَبَّهُ إِنِّي أَخَافُ أَن يُبَدِّلَ دِينَكُمْ أَوْ أَن يُظْهِرَ فِي الْأَرْضِ الْفَسَادَ

And said Fira'on, leave me (let me that) I kill (prophet) Musa (peace be upon him and he should (let him) call (invoke) Lord of his (Allah), surely I (Fira'on) fear (am afraid) that he (prophet Musa peace be upon him) will change Deen (religion, tradition, way of life) of yours or that he will make evident in the earth mischief (corruption, disorganization)

Aya 49:27

وَقَالَ مُوسَىٰ إِنِّي عُذْتُ بِرَبِّي وَرَبِّكُم مِّن كُلِّ مُتَكَبِّرٍ لَّا يُؤْمِنُ بِيَوْمِ الْحِسَابِ

And said (prophet) Musa (peace be upon him), surely, I have sought refuge on (with) Lord of mine (Allah) and Lord of yours (Allah) from every (all) arrogant (proud person) not believing on the day of the accounts (day of judgment)

Revelation Background

1. The following few Aya mention the story of a Momin (true believer) person from the family or people of Fir'aon

2. This Momin (true believer) person was hiding his eman (true belief) and was helping prophet Musa peace be upon him in so many different ways

3. This Surah is named after that Momin person as Surah Al Momin. Other name for this Surah is Surah Al Ghafir

4. It is permitted to hide your true beliefs in situations like those mentioned in these Aya

5. Guidance and eman (true belief) is with the mercy of Allah. True believers may be hidden amongst a non-believer nation or crowd

6. Eman and true belief is ultimately an individual issue in the heart of one person and is not a family, tribal, national or crowd issue

7. Group labels or blanket blame may not be accurate, many of the times

Aya 40:28

وَقَالَ رَجُلٌ مُّؤْمِنٌ مِّنْ آلِ فِرْعَوْنَ يَكْتُمُ إِيمَانَهُ أَتَقْتُلُونَ رَجُلًا أَن يَقُولَ رَبِّيَ اللَّهُ وَقَدْ جَاءَكُم بِالْبَيِّنَاتِ مِن رَّبِّكُمْ وَإِن يَكُ كَاذِبًا فَعَلَيْهِ كَذِبُهُ وَإِن يَكُ صَادِقًا يُصِبْكُم بَعْضُ الَّذِي يَعِدُكُمْ إِنَّ اللَّهَ لَا يَهْدِي مَنْ هُوَ مُسْرِفٌ كَذَّابٌ

And said the man Momin (a true believer in Allah and Islam) from the family of Fir'aon, he was hiding eman (true belief in Allah) of his, (he said to his people) "are you killing a man (referring to prophet Musa peace be upon him) that he says, the Lord of mine is Allah and surely he (prophet Musa peace be upon him) came to you on (with) clear evidences, from the Lord of yours (Allah)? And if he (prophet Musa peace be upon him) be a liar, so on him will be (the punishment) of the lie of his and if he (prophet Musa peace be upon him) be truthful, will reach you (as affliction) some of what (punishment of Allah) he is promising you, surely Allah does not guide the one who is extravagant (transgressor), severe liar."

Aya 40:29

يَا قَوْمِ لَكُمُ الْمُلْكُ الْيَوْمَ ظَاهِرِينَ فِي الْأَرْضِ فَمَن يَنصُرُنَا مِن بَأْسِ اللَّهِ إِن جَاءَنَا قَالَ فِرْعَوْنُ مَا أُرِيكُمْ إِلَّا مَا أَرَىٰ وَمَا أَهْدِيكُمْ إِلَّا سَبِيلَ الرَّشَادِ

(The true believer man said), O my nation (people), for you is the kingdom (authority) this day, dominators (topmost, prevailing) in the earth (land), so who will help (save) us from the punishment of Allah if it (the punishment of Allah) came to us, said Fira'on, not I show you except what I see and not I guide you except the path of the righteousness (correct path)

Aya 40:30

وَقَالَ الَّذِي آمَنَ يَا قَوْمِ إِنِّي أَخَافُ عَلَيْكُم مِّثْلَ يَوْمِ الْأَحْزَابِ

And said the one who believed (in Allah, the true Momin man), O my nation (people), surely, I fear on you (against you) like the example of the day of (punishment of the) groups (before you, nations before you)

Aya 40:31

مِثْلَ دَأْبِ قَوْمِ نُوحٍ وَعَادٍ وَثَمُودَ وَالَّذِينَ مِن بَعْدِهِمْ وَمَا اللَّهُ يُرِيدُ ظُلْمًا لِّلْعِبَادِ

Like the fate (manner, custom) of the nation of (prophet) Nuh (peace be upon him) and (nation of) A'ad and (nation of) Thamud and those (people who came) from after them, and not is Allah, intending oppression (injustice) for (His) servants.

Aya 40:32

وَيَا قَوْمِ إِنِّي أَخَافُ عَلَيْكُمْ يَوْمَ التَّنَادِ

(True believer man said) And, O nation (people) of mine, surely I fear on you (against you) the day of the calling (day of resurrection, when people will be resurrected with the sound or call of the trumpet blown into by the angel Israfeel, or will be calling each other or will be calling for help due to terror of that day)

Aya 40:33

يَوْمَ تُوَلُّونَ مُدْبِرِينَ مَا لَكُم مِّنَ اللَّهِ مِنْ عَاصِمٍ وَمَن يُضْلِلِ اللَّهُ فَمَا لَهُ مِنْ هَادٍ

The day you will be turning away, making your backs (going back from the place of accounts to the hellfire or trying to runway from the punishment), not will be there for you, from (the punishment of) Allah from any protector (savior), and the one (who) Allah put astray, so not is there for him, from (any) guider.

Aya 40:34

وَلَقَدْ جَاءَكُمْ يُوسُفُ مِن قَبْلُ بِالْبَيِّنَاتِ فَمَا زِلْتُمْ فِي شَكٍّ مِّمَّا جَاءَكُم بِهِ ۖ حَتَّىٰ إِذَا هَلَكَ قُلْتُمْ لَن يَبْعَثَ اللَّهُ مِن بَعْدِهِ رَسُولًا ۚ كَذَٰلِكَ يُضِلُّ اللَّهُ مَنْ هُوَ مُسْرِفٌ مُّرْتَابٌ

And surely, came to you (prophet) Yousuf (peace be upon him) from before (before prophet Musa peace be upon him) with clear evidences, so not you stopped (ceased) to be in doubt (you remained in doubt, you did not cease to be in doubt) from what he came to you on it (the message of Allah), till he (prophet Yousuf peace be upon him) died, you said never will send Allah from after him (after prophet Yousuf peace be upon him, another) messenger, like that put astray Allah, the one (who) is extravagant (transgressor), doubter (skeptic)

Aya 40:35

الَّذِينَ يُجَادِلُونَ فِي آيَاتِ اللَّهِ بِغَيْرِ سُلْطَانٍ أَتَاهُمْ ۖ كَبُرَ مَقْتًا عِندَ اللَّهِ وَعِندَ الَّذِينَ آمَنُوا ۚ كَذَٰلِكَ يَطْبَعُ اللَّهُ عَلَىٰ كُلِّ قَلْبِ مُتَكَبِّرٍ جَبَّارٍ

Those (people who) are quarreling (fighting, disputing) in signs of Allah (verses of Allah), without (any) authority (authentic evidence or knowledge) that came to them, (that dispute without evidence) is big in displeasure (hatred, disgust) with (in the sight of) Allah and with those (people who) believed, like that put seal (of disbelief) Allah on every (all) heart arrogant and tyrant (compeller, high-handed, forcing people)

Aya 40:36

وَقَالَ فِرْعَوْنُ يَا هَامَانُ ابْنِ لِي صَرْحًا لَّعَلِّي أَبْلُغُ الْأَسْبَابَ

And said Fir'aon, "O Haamaan (his deputy) build for me a palace (high tower), perhaps I may reach the means (ways to access)"

Aya 40:37

أَسْبَابَ السَّمَاوَاتِ فَأَطَّلِعَ إِلَىٰ إِلَٰهِ مُوسَىٰ وَإِنِّي لَأَظُنُّهُ كَاذِبًا ۚ وَكَذَٰلِكَ زُيِّنَ لِفِرْعَوْنَ سُوءُ عَمَلِهِ وَصُدَّ عَنِ السَّبِيلِ ۚ وَمَا كَيْدُ فِرْعَوْنَ إِلَّا فِي تَبَابٍ

Means of (access to) the skies (heavens) so I may look at (get information on) God of (prophet) Musa (peace be upon him) and surely I, definitely, suppose (think of him, consider) him (as a) liar, and like that, were made beautiful for Fir'aon bad deed of his and was prevented (stopped) from the path (correct path of Allah) and not was the plan (trick) of Fir'aon except in destruction (ruins)

Aya 40:38

وَقَالَ الَّذِي آمَنَ يَا قَوْمِ اتَّبِعُونِ أَهْدِكُمْ سَبِيلَ الرَّشَادِ

And said the one who believed (the true Momin man), O my nation (people), follow me, I will guide you, to the path of the correctness (the true guidance)

Aya 40:39

يَا قَوْمِ إِنَّمَا هَٰذِهِ الْحَيَاةُ الدُّنْيَا مَتَاعٌ وَإِنَّ الْآخِرَةَ هِيَ دَارُ الْقَرَارِ

O my nation (people), surely this, the life of the world, is (a) benefit (temporary small enjoyment) and surely, the later (the hereafter), it is the home of the settlement (living forever, settled and satisfied)

Aya 40:40

مَنْ عَمِلَ سَيِّئَةً فَلَا يُجْزَىٰ إِلَّا مِثْلَهَا وَمَنْ عَمِلَ صَالِحًا مِّن ذَكَرٍ أَوْ أُنثَىٰ وَهُوَ مُؤْمِنٌ فَأُولَٰئِكَ يَدْخُلُونَ الْجَنَّةَ يُرْزَقُونَ فِيهَا بِغَيْرِ حِسَابٍ

The one who did (a) bad deed, so not will he be rewarded (punished for his bad deed) except like it (equal to his bad deed), and the one who did (a) good deed, from male or female and he is Momin (true believer), so those (people) will enter the Garden (paradise), they will be provided sustenance (food and enjoyment) in it (in paradise) without accounts (without limits)

Aya 40:41

وَيَا قَوْمِ مَا لِي أَدْعُوكُمْ إِلَى النَّجَاةِ وَتَدْعُونَنِي إِلَى النَّارِ

And O my nation (people), what is for me (that) I am calling you (inviting you) toward liberation (safeguarding you from hellfire, salvation), and you are calling me (inviting me) toward the fire (hellfire)

Aya 40:42

تَدْعُونَنِي لِأَكْفُرَ بِاللَّهِ وَأُشْرِكَ بِهِ مَا لَيْسَ لِي بِهِ عِلْمٌ وَأَنَا أَدْعُوكُمْ إِلَى الْعَزِيزِ الْغَفَّارِ

(Momin man said, O my people) You are calling (inviting) me, for me to reject (disbelieve) on Allah and (that) I make partners with Him (with Allah) what (false gods), not is there for me on it (on making partners gods, any) knowledge and I call (invite) you toward (only One Allah) the All-Mighty, the Most-Forgiver (Allah)

Aya 40:43

لَا جَرَمَ أَنَّمَا تَدْعُونَنِي إِلَيْهِ لَيْسَ لَهُ دَعْوَةٌ فِي الدُّنْيَا وَلَا فِي الْآخِرَةِ وَأَنَّ مَرَدَّنَا إِلَى اللَّهِ وَأَنَّ الْمُسْرِفِينَ هُمْ أَصْحَابُ النَّارِ

No doubt (it is obvious) that what you are calling (inviting) me toward it (false gods), not is there for him (for false gods, any response to) calling (invocation and supplications) in the world and not in the hereafter and that return of ours is toward Allah (on the day of judgment) and that the extravagant (transgressors), they are companions of the fire (hellfire)

Aya 40:44

فَسَتَذْكُرُونَ مَا أَقُولُ لَكُمْ وَأُفَوِّضُ أَمْرِي إِلَى اللَّهِ إِنَّ اللَّهَ بَصِيرٌ بِالْعِبَادِ

So, you will remember what I say for you, and I entrust (delegate) affairs of mine toward Allah, surely, Allah is All-Seer on (His) servants.

Aya 40:45

فَوَقَاهُ اللَّهُ سَيِّئَاتِ مَا مَكَرُوا وَحَاقَ بِآلِ فِرْعَوْنَ سُوءُ الْعَذَابِ

So, protected (saved) him (the true believer man) Allah from bad deeds (plots), what they (people of Fir'aon) plotted (planned against him) and befell (encompassed) on family (people) of Fir'aon, bad of the punishment.

Aya 40:46

النَّارُ يُعْرَضُونَ عَلَيْهَا غُدُوًّا وَعَشِيًّا وَيَوْمَ تَقُومُ السَّاعَةُ أَدْخِلُوا آلَ فِرْعَوْنَ أَشَدَّ الْعَذَابِ

The (punishment of) fire, they (the people of Fir'aon) are presented on it (on that fire), morning and evening and the day, (when) will be established, the hour (of judgment), (will be said), enter family (people) of Fir'aon, the most intense of the punishment.

Aya 40:47

وَإِذْ يَتَحَاجُّونَ فِي النَّارِ فَيَقُولُ الضُّعَفَاءُ لِلَّذِينَ اسْتَكْبَرُوا إِنَّا كُنَّا لَكُمْ تَبَعًا فَهَلْ أَنتُم مُّغْنُونَ عَنَّا نَصِيبًا مِّنَ النَّارِ

And, when they will be arguing (while they are) in the fire, so will say the weak (people who followed their leaders in bad deeds) for those (people who) practiced arrogance (arrogant leaders in the world), surely, we were for you followers (in the worldly life), so are you saviors (to take away) from us (a) portion from (punishment of) the fire?

Aya 40:48

قَالَ الَّذِينَ اسْتَكْبَرُوا إِنَّا كُلٌّ فِيهَا إِنَّ اللَّهَ قَدْ حَكَمَ بَيْنَ الْعِبَادِ

Said those (people who) practiced arrogance (the arrogant leaders in the world),. surely, we all are in it (in the punishment of fire), surely, Allah definitely decided between his servants.

Aya 40:49

وَقَالَ الَّذِينَ فِي النَّارِ لِخَزَنَةِ جَهَنَّمَ ادْعُوا رَبَّكُمْ يُخَفِّفْ عَنَّا يَوْمًا مِّنَ الْعَذَابِ

And said, those (people) who are in the fire, for the keepers (guards) of hell, call (pray to) Lord of yours (Allah), to lighten (reduce) from us (a) day from the punishment.

Aya 40:50

قَالُوا أَوَلَمْ تَكُ تَأْتِيكُمْ رُسُلُكُم بِالْبَيِّنَاتِ قَالُوا بَلَىٰ قَالُوا فَادْعُوا وَمَا دُعَاءُ الْكَافِرِينَ إِلَّا فِي ضَلَالٍ

They (guards of the hell) said, were not coming to you (in the worldly life) messengers of yours (peace be upon all of them, from Allah) on clear evidences?, they (residents of hell) said, "Yes, (came to us messengers, peace be upon all of them), they (guards of hell) said, so you call (pray yourselves) and not is the call (prayers) of the disbelievers except in error (lost, in vain)

Aya 40:51

إِنَّا لَنَنصُرُ رُسُلَنَا وَالَّذِينَ آمَنُوا فِي الْحَيَاةِ الدُّنْيَا وَيَوْمَ يَقُومُ الْأَشْهَادُ

Surely, We (Allah), definitely, We (Allah) help messengers (peace be upon them) of Ours (of Allah) and (Allah helps) those (people) who believed (Allah), in the (during the) life of the world and (Allah helps them on) the day (when) will stand the witnesses (for accounts on the day of judgment)

Aya 40:52

يَوْمَ لَا يَنفَعُ الظَّالِمِينَ مَعْذِرَتُهُمْ وَلَهُمُ اللَّعْنَةُ وَلَهُمْ سُوءُ الدَّارِ

The day (when will stand the witnesses, the day of judgment), not will benefit the oppressors (unjust people) excuse of theirs and for them is the curse (repulsion from Allah's mercy) and for them (for unjust, oppressors) will be bad of the home (residence in hellfire)

Aya 40:53

وَلَقَدْ آتَيْنَا مُوسَى الْهُدَىٰ وَأَوْرَثْنَا بَنِي إِسْرَائِيلَ الْكِتَابَ

And surely, We (Allah) gave (prophet) Musa (peace be upon him) the guidance, and We (Allah) gave (in) inheritance to Children of Israel, the book (Thoraat)

Aya 40:54

هُدًى وَذِكْرَىٰ لِأُولِي الْأَلْبَابِ

(That book of Thoraat, was) A guidance and a remembrance (reminder) for the owners (people) of the wit (intelligence, understanding, intellect, wisdom)

Aya 40:55

فَاصْبِرْ إِنَّ وَعْدَ اللَّهِ حَقٌّ وَاسْتَغْفِرْ لِذَنبِكَ وَسَبِّحْ بِحَمْدِ رَبِّكَ بِالْعَشِيِّ وَالْإِبْكَارِ

So, practice patience, surely, the promise of Allah is true, and seek forgiveness for sin of yours and proclaim purity on (with) praise of Lord of yours, on the evening and the early (morning)

Aya 40:56

إِنَّ الَّذِينَ يُجَادِلُونَ فِي آيَاتِ اللَّهِ بِغَيْرِ سُلْطَانٍ أَتَاهُمْ إِن فِي صُدُورِهِمْ إِلَّا كِبْرٌ مَّا هُم بِبَالِغِيهِ فَاسْتَعِذْ بِاللَّهِ إِنَّهُ هُوَ السَّمِيعُ الْبَصِيرُ

Surely, those who quarrel (argue, dispute) in signs (verses) of Allah, without (any) authority (authentic knowledge that) came to them, not is in chests (hearts) of theirs except arrogance (pride), not are they reacher (achievers) of it (of their arrogance), so seek refuge on (with) Allah, surely He (Allah) is the All-Listener the All-Seer

Aya 40:57

لَخَلْقُ السَّمَاوَاتِ وَالْأَرْضِ أَكْبَرُ مِنْ خَلْقِ النَّاسِ وَلَٰكِنَّ أَكْثَرَ النَّاسِ لَا يَعْلَمُونَ

Definitely, the creation of the skies (heavens) and the earth is greater (bigger, vaster and more complex) from (than) the creation of the people, but the majority (most) of the people, not they know.

Aya 40:58

وَمَا يَسْتَوِي الْأَعْمَىٰ وَالْبَصِيرُ وَالَّذِينَ آمَنُوا وَعَمِلُوا الصَّالِحَاتِ وَلَا الْمُسِيءُ قَلِيلًا مَّا تَتَذَكَّرُونَ

And not are equal, the blind and the seer and (not are equal) those who believed, and they did good deeds and not the evil-doer (those doing bad deeds), little is what you take remembrance (lesson, reminder)

Aya 40:59

إِنَّ السَّاعَةَ لَآتِيَةٌ لَا رَيْبَ فِيهَا وَلَٰكِنَّ أَكْثَرَ النَّاسِ لَا يُؤْمِنُونَ

Surely, the hour (day of judgment), definitely, is coming, not is there (any) doubt in it (in coming of the day of judgment), but the majority (most) of the people, not they believe.

Aya 40:60

وَقَالَ رَبُّكُمُ ادْعُونِي أَسْتَجِبْ لَكُمْ إِنَّ الَّذِينَ يَسْتَكْبِرُونَ عَنْ عِبَادَتِي سَيَدْخُلُونَ جَهَنَّمَ دَاخِرِينَ

And said Lord of yours (Allah), call (pray, invoke) Me (Allah), I will answer (respond, reply, acknowledge) for you, surely those who are practicing arrogance from worship of Mine (not praying to only One Allah), soon they will enter the hell, disgraced (humiliated)

Aya 40:61

اللَّهُ الَّذِي جَعَلَ لَكُمُ اللَّيْلَ لِتَسْكُنُوا فِيهِ وَالنَّهَارَ مُبْصِرًا إِنَّ اللَّهَ لَذُو فَضْلٍ عَلَى النَّاسِ وَلَٰكِنَّ أَكْثَرَ النَّاسِ لَا يَشْكُرُونَ

Allah is the One who made for you the night, so you may rest in it (at night) and the day seer (bright and showing you everything out there). Surely, Allah, definitely is, the Owner of bounty (giving, grace) on the people, but the majority (most) of the people, not they give thanks (offer gratitude to Allah)

Aya 40:62

ذَٰلِكُمُ اللَّهُ رَبُّكُمْ خَالِقُ كُلِّ شَيْءٍ لَا إِلَٰهَ إِلَّا هُوَ فَأَنَّىٰ تُؤْفَكُونَ

That you (to know), Allah is Lord of yours, Creator of every (all) thing, not is there any one worthy of worship except Him (except Allah), so where are you led to falsehood (deluded, put astray)

Aya 40:63

كَذَٰلِكَ يُؤْفَكُ الَّذِينَ كَانُوا بِآيَاتِ اللَّهِ يَجْحَدُونَ

Like that, are led to falsehood (deluded, put astray) those who were on signs (verses) of Allah, denying (rejecting).

Aya 40:64

اللَّهُ الَّذِي جَعَلَ لَكُمُ الْأَرْضَ قَرَارًا وَالسَّمَاءَ بِنَاءً وَصَوَّرَكُمْ فَأَحْسَنَ صُوَرَكُمْ وَرَزَقَكُم مِّنَ الطَّيِّبَاتِ ذَٰلِكُمُ اللَّهُ رَبُّكُمْ فَتَبَارَكَ اللَّهُ رَبُّ الْعَالَمِينَ

Allah is the One who made for you the earth as the place of settlement (stability, dwelling) and the sky (heaven as) a building (canopy, ceiling), and He (Allah) shaped you so He (Allah) made better shapes of yours and He (Allah) provided sustenance (food and provisions) to you from the clean (good) foods (good things), that (for) you, is the Allah, Lord of yours, so blessed is Allah, Lord of the universes.

Aya 40:65

هُوَ الْحَيُّ لَا إِلَٰهَ إِلَّا هُوَ فَادْعُوهُ مُخْلِصِينَ لَهُ الدِّينَ الْحَمْدُ لِلَّهِ رَبِّ الْعَالَمِينَ

He (Allah) is The Ever-Living, not is there any one worthy of worship except Him (Allah), so call (invoke, pray to) Him (Allah), making pure (exclusive, sincere) for Him (for Allah) the deen (religion, worship, the way of life), the (all and total) praise is (only) for Allah, the Lord of the universes.

Aya 40:66

قُلْ إِنِّي نُهِيتُ أَنْ أَعْبُدَ الَّذِينَ تَدْعُونَ مِن دُونِ اللَّهِ لَمَّا جَاءَنِيَ الْبَيِّنَاتُ مِن رَّبِّي وَأُمِرْتُ أَنْ أُسْلِمَ لِرَبِّ الْعَالَمِينَ

Say (O prophet Muhammad, peace be upon him), surely, I am forbidden (prohibited by Allah from) that I worship those (gods) who you are calling (invoking, praying to) from besides (other than) Allah, (after) when came to me the clear evidences (Quran) from Lord of mine (Allah) and I am ordered (commanded by Allah) that I submit (obey and worship only) for Lord of the universes (Allah.)

Aya 40:67

هُوَ الَّذِي خَلَقَكُم مِّن تُرَابٍ ثُمَّ مِن نُّطْفَةٍ ثُمَّ مِنْ عَلَقَةٍ ثُمَّ يُخْرِجُكُمْ طِفْلًا ثُمَّ لِتَبْلُغُوا أَشُدَّكُمْ ثُمَّ لِتَكُونُوا شُيُوخًا وَمِنكُم مَّن يُتَوَفَّىٰ مِن قَبْلُ وَلِتَبْلُغُوا أَجَلًا مُّسَمًّى وَلَعَلَّكُمْ تَعْقِلُونَ

(Lord of universes, Allah) He is the One, who created you from dust (originally from clay), then from (a) drop of semen, then from a clot, then He (Allah) gets you out (from the womb) as a child, then for you to reach intensity (power and strength) of yours, then for you to become old (men and women) and (some) from you, the one who are made to die from before (without getting old) and for you to reach an appointed time (for death already) named and perhaps you may use your wit (intelligence, understanding)

Aya 40:68

هُوَ الَّذِي يُحْيِي وَيُمِيتُ ۖ فَإِذَا قَضَىٰ أَمْرًا فَإِنَّمَا يَقُولُ لَهُ كُنْ فَيَكُونُ

He (Allah) is the One (Allah who) gives life and gives death, so when He (Allah) decides an issue (an order, an affair), so surely, He (Allah) says to it (to that issue) get done, so it gets done

Aya 40:69

أَلَمْ تَرَ إِلَى الَّذِينَ يُجَادِلُونَ فِي آيَاتِ اللَّهِ أَنَّىٰ يُصْرَفُونَ

Did you not see (consider, think), toward those who are quarreling (arguing disputing) in signs (verses) of Allah? So where are they turned away (diverted away from the truth)?

Aya 40:70

الَّذِينَ كَذَّبُوا بِالْكِتَابِ وَبِمَا أَرْسَلْنَا بِهِ رُسُلَنَا ۖ فَسَوْفَ يَعْلَمُونَ

Those (people) who belied (rejected) on the Book (of Allah) and on what We (Allah) sent on it (message of Islam) messengers (peace be upon all of them) of Ours (Allah), so soon, they will know (consequences of their rejection)

Aya 40:71

إِذِ الْأَغْلَالُ فِي أَعْنَاقِهِمْ وَالسَّلَاسِلُ يُسْحَبُونَ

When the shackles (fetters will be) in necks of theirs and the chains, they (disbelievers) will be dragged (pulled)

Aya 40:72

فِي الْحَمِيمِ ثُمَّ فِي النَّارِ يُسْجَرُونَ

In the boiling water, then in the fire, they will be fueled (thrown into hellfire as fuel, or they will be filled in the hell)

Aya 40:73

ثُمَّ قِيلَ لَهُمْ أَيْنَ مَا كُنْتُمْ تُشْرِكُونَ

Then, said for them (residents of hell), where are what (false gods) you were associating (as partners with Allah)?

Aya 40:74

مِن دُونِ اللَّهِ قَالُوا ضَلُّوا عَنَّا بَل لَّمْ نَكُن نَّدْعُو مِن قَبْلُ شَيْئًا كَذَٰلِكَ يُضِلُّ اللَّهُ الْكَافِرِينَ

(Where are those false gods) From besides (other than) Allah, they (residents of hell) said, got lost from us (those false gods), but (no, no, rather) not were, we calling (in prayers, worshiping) from before anything, like that puts astray, Allah, the disbelievers.

Aya 40:75

ذَٰلِكُم بِمَا كُنتُمْ تَفْرَحُونَ فِي الْأَرْضِ بِغَيْرِ الْحَقِّ وَبِمَا كُنتُمْ تَمْرَحُونَ

That (punishment for) you, is on (because of) what you were rejoicing (were happy and elated in arrogance) in the earth without the truth (were happy with falsehood) and on (because of) what you were acting arrogantly (in the worldly life)

Aya 40:76

ادْخُلُوا أَبْوَابَ جَهَنَّمَ خَالِدِينَ فِيهَا فَبِئْسَ مَثْوَى الْمُتَكَبِّرِينَ

Enter gates of the hell, stayer forever in it (in hell), so, bad is the place of living of the arrogant (people)

Aya 40:77

فَاصْبِرْ إِنَّ وَعْدَ اللَّهِ حَقٌّ فَإِمَّا نُرِيَنَّكَ بَعْضَ الَّذِي نَعِدُهُمْ أَوْ نَتَوَفَّيَنَّكَ فَإِلَيْنَا يُرْجَعُونَ

So, practice patience (O prophet Muhammad, peace be upon him), surely, the promise of Allah is true, so either We (Allah) will show you (in your lifetime, O prophet Muhammad, peace be upon him) some of the one (punishment) We (Allah) promise them (disbelievers) or We (Allah) will make you die (fulfill your lifetime before their punishment), so toward Us (toward Allah) they will be returned (for ultimate punishment)

Aya 40:78

وَلَقَدْ أَرْسَلْنَا رُسُلًا مِّن قَبْلِكَ مِنْهُم مَّن قَصَصْنَا عَلَيْكَ وَمِنْهُم مَّن لَّمْ نَقْصُصْ عَلَيْكَ وَمَا كَانَ لِرَسُولٍ أَن يَأْتِيَ بِآيَةٍ إِلَّا بِإِذْنِ اللَّهِ فَإِذَا جَاءَ أَمْرُ اللَّهِ قُضِيَ بِالْحَقِّ وَخَسِرَ هُنَالِكَ الْمُبْطِلُونَ

And surely, We (Allah) sent messengers (peace be upon all of them) from before you (O prophet Muhammad, peace be upon him), from them (from those earlier messengers) are the one (s) We (Allah) mentioned stories (of theirs) on you and from them are the one (s), not We (Allah) mentioned stories (of theirs) on you and not is (allowed) for a messenger (peace be upon all of them), that he brings on any sign (miracle) except on the permission of Allah, so when came order (command) of Allah (for the punishment of the rejectors of those prophets peace be upon all of them), got decided (the matter of their punishment) on the truth (justice) and lost there, the falsifiers (deniers and rejectors were losers)

Aya 40:79

اللَّهُ الَّذِي جَعَلَ لَكُمُ الْأَنْعَامَ لِتَرْكَبُوا مِنْهَا وَمِنْهَا تَأْكُلُونَ

Allah is the One, He (Allah) made (created) for you, the cattle (s), for you to ride from it (from some of the cattle), and from it (from some of cattle) you eat.

Aya 40:80

وَلَكُمْ فِيهَا مَنَافِعُ وَلِتَبْلُغُوا عَلَيْهَا حَاجَةً فِي صُدُورِكُمْ وَعَلَيْهَا وَعَلَى الْفُلْكِ تُحْمَلُونَ

And for you, in it (in cattle) are (many) benefits and for you to reach on (backs of) it (cattle) a need (wish for transportation) in the chest (hearts) of yours and on it (on cattle) and on the ships, you are loaded (carried, loaded for reaching from one place to another)

Aya 40:81

وَيُرِيكُمْ آيَاتِهِ فَأَيَّ آيَاتِ اللَّهِ تُنكِرُونَ

And He (Allah) shows you signs of His (Allah), so on which (of the) signs of Allah, are you refuting (denying, is strange for you, not recognizing it)?

Aya 40:82

أَفَلَمْ يَسِيرُوا فِي الْأَرْضِ فَيَنظُرُوا كَيْفَ كَانَ عَاقِبَةُ الَّذِينَ مِن قَبْلِهِمْ كَانُوا أَكْثَرَ مِنْهُمْ وَأَشَدَّ قُوَّةً وَآثَارًا فِي الْأَرْضِ فَمَا أَغْنَىٰ عَنْهُم مَّا كَانُوا يَكْسِبُونَ

Did not they (disbelievers) travel in the earth? So they may see, how was the final status (end outcome) of those (people) from before them? They (those previous people) were more (in number) from them (as compared to current disbelievers) and were more intense in power and in footprints (signs, impact) in the earth, so not saved (benefited, removed punishment of Allah) from them what they (those previously destroyed nations) were earning (doing)

Aya 40:83

فَلَمَّا جَاءَتْهُمْ رُسُلُهُم بِالْبَيِّنَاتِ فَرِحُوا بِمَا عِندَهُم مِّنَ الْعِلْمِ وَحَاقَ بِهِم مَّا كَانُوا بِهِ يَسْتَهْزِئُونَ

So, when came to them (to those previously destroyed nations) messengers (of Allah, peace be upon all of them) of theirs, on clear evidences (from Allah), they got happy (arrogantly) on what was with them from the knowledge and encircled (befell, came down) on them what (punishment of Allah) they were on it, joking (mocking)

Aya 40:84

فَلَمَّا رَأَوْا بَأْسَنَا قَالُوا آمَنَّا بِاللَّهِ وَحْدَهُ وَكَفَرْنَا بِمَا كُنَّا بِهِ مُشْرِكِينَ

So, when they (those previously destroyed nations) saw (the) punishment of Ours (Allah), they said, we believed on Allah alone, and we rejected on what we were on Him (on Allah) associators (as false partners with Allah)

Aya 40:85

فَلَمْ يَكُ يَنفَعُهُمْ إِيمَانُهُمْ لَمَّا رَأَوْا بَأْسَنَا سُنَّتَ اللَّهِ الَّتِي قَدْ خَلَتْ فِي عِبَادِهِ وَخَسِرَ هُنَالِكَ الْكَافِرُونَ

So, not was to benefit (save) them (last minute) belief of theirs, when they saw the punishment of Ours (Allah), tradition (established way and pattern) of Allah, the one (tradition), surely, passed (preceded before) in servants of His (of Allah) and lost (became losers) there the disbelievers.

www.ingramcontent.com/pod-product-compliance
Lightning Source LLC
Chambersburg PA
CBHW081711100526
44590CB00022B/3738